THE POETRY WITCH
LITTLE BOOK
OF
LOVE POEMS

# THE POETRY WITCH
# LITTLE BOOK
# OF
# LOVE POEMS

BY ANNIE FINCH

POETRY WITCH PRESS

Poetry Witch Press
Brooklyn, NY, USA
www.anniefinch.com

© 2025 Poetry Witch Press
All rights reserved

Book design by Sophia Renda

9781737307594

*For Glen*

# CONTENTS

Courtship .................................................10

Two Bodies .................................................11

Love in the Morning .................................12

Conversation .................................................13

Earth Goddess and Sky God .................................14

Landing Under Water, I See Roots .................15

Dusk Song .................................................16

Turn .................................................17

Death and the Mountain .................................18

Your Forest .................................................19

## COURTSHIP

Courtship is pulling with your full-moon heart
to bring out patterns. Patterns dry, crisp tides
that crescent up the beach, past sifted sand,
as sunset comes. When all the shores are dark,
night pulls with courtship's tides (Love leaves the tides
aside, to push on further up the sand,
to change far pools, to ebb into the heart
of earth and leave it salty, full, and dark).

## TWO BODIES

Two bodies, balanced in mass and power,
move in a bed through the dark,
under the earliest human hour.
A night rocks, like an ark.

They reach through the ceilings of the night,
tall as animals.
Through their valleys bends the light
of their fertile hills.

Two bodies breathe their close hellos
through interlocking pores,
while that hush of beating slows,
held by many oars.

Heart over heart, leg over leg,
trading still breath, until,
heart over heart, and seed into egg,
night holds two bodies still.

## LOVE IN THE MORNING

Morning's a new bird
stirring against me
out of a quiet nest,
coming to flight—

quick-changing,
slow-nodding,
breath-filling body,

life-holding,
waiting,
clean as clear water,

warmth-given,
fire-driven
kindling companion,

mystery and mountain,
dark-rooted,
earth-anchored.

## CONVERSATION

*(Edward Weston's "Squash," 1936)*

"Delve for me, delve down, delve past your body, crowned
by its hidden stem, like a shadowy alarm;
see how you vanish past our dark-shed charm,
throat over throat, ankle to ankle, bound
in our different arches, summer-nicked and browned
interlocking rings in the chain of wrist and arm."

"Lie for me, lie. I want to feel you turn.
Mark out the summer's bending month and learn
to cradle the concrete ground till it softens. Stay.
Measure me past my stem. Though your shadows churn,
close yourself over. Encompass me like clay."

# EARTH GODDESS & SKY GOD

You haven't formed me. I'm a monster still.
Then give me your body. Give it to me in rain.
Look up and fill me. I am too dark to stain.
You haven't held me. I hold apart my will.
Spread dryness through me. I have a night to fill
in high heat-speckled waves, apart from where
I will come down. I have nothing to share
with breath. I will give it back. There is one to kill,
one to renew, and one to persuade to weep.
My night holds everything except for sleep.

# LANDING UNDER WATER, I SEE ROOTS

All the things we hide in water
hoping we won't see them go—
(forests growing under water
press against the ones we know)—

and they might have gone on growing
and they might now breathe above
everything I speak of sowing
(everything I try to love).

## DUSK SONG

Over the big bed in the small room
The flat shadow
Turned, thinning our walls
Insistently,
Turning and turning us closer and closer to salt wind
In from the sea.

I could sing a song about a long gone lover,
Cape Cod dusk, Cape Cod shadow;
I sang a song then about the Cape Cod shadow,
Over door and wall, over
Shoulder and shoulder.

Did I have a face and did it lie
In shadow
Turning and turning your glances away?

Once there was a song about the Cape Cod shadow;
I sang the song.
The flat shadow turned over our walls and brought the sea in.
The song kept turning.

# TURN

Here in the dark, to be with you
Is to be like a candle flame
Making long meadows in the night
Across which I can call your name.

Will you turn and be with me,
Walking to meet me in the sun
That colors all the grass-tops brown
With building harvests not yet done?

I will turn.  I'll meet you there.
Across the night I'll find your hand.
Together we will turn, alone,
out from the candle and the land.

# DEATH AND THE MOUNTAIN

You're like a mountain made of warmth
That births a river made of touch
Where stones of time have tumbled forth
Catching the light that loves so much.
The dark that loves is what we feel,
However, in our nighttime path.
Look how open and bright she comes
Together with us, coming death!
She is the mother in the rose,
The burrow, and the sainted breath.

## YOUR FOREST

Your forest goes as green as love;
your ferns are dappled near the ground,
and moss they dappled curls above
stones that your glacier dappled down.

Your night is sadness well-contained
within the sap that runs the stem
of plants that grow along the night
and root at morning. Joy finds them,

and oceans, lost because they are vast
(like ruined roads left on the land)
take your kind waters home each time
that they, pushing raptly at the sand,

make tides with your evaporate rain.
The ocean is at peace again.
Far algae grows, the blue stays smooth,
and in dim light, the beach is soothed.

Your forest goes as green as love,
your night is sadness well-contained,
and oceans, lost because they are vast,
make tides with your evaporate rain.

# ACKNOWLEDGEMENTS

"Courtship," first collected in *Eve* (Story Line Press, 1997, Reprinted by Carnegie Mellon University Press Contemporary Classics Poetry Series, 2011)

"Death and the Mountain," first published in *Rattle*

"Earth Goddess and Sky God," first collected in *Calendars* (Tupelo Press, 2003, second edition with CD, 2008)

"Conversation," first collected in *Calendars* (Tupelo Press, 2003, second edition with CD, 2008).

"Landing Under Water, I See Roots," first collected in *Calendars* (Tupelo Press, 2003, second edition with CD, 2008)

"Dusk Song," composed in 1978, first published in *Spells: New and Selected Poems* (Wesleyan University Press, 2013)

"Love in the Morning," first appeared on Academy of American Poets Website

"Your Forest," first published in *National Poetry Review*

"Two Bodies," first collected in *Calendars* (Tupelo Press, 2003, second edition with CD, 2008)

"Turn," first published in *Spells: New and Selected Poems* (Wesleyan University Press, 2013)

# ABOUT THE POET

Annie Finch is the author of seven volumes of poetry, including *Calendars* and *Eve*, both finalists for the National Poetry Series, and *Spells: New and Selected Poems* (Wesleyan University Press). Her poetry has been featured in periodicals such as the *New York Times, Poetry Magazine,* and *The Paris Review* and books such as *The Penguin Book of Twentieth-Century American Poetry, Penguin Book of the Sonnet,* and *Norton Anthology of World Literature*. Finch is also the author of *A Poet's Craft: A Comprehensive Guide to Making and Sharing Your Poetry* and editor of ten anthologies including *A Formal Feeling Comes, Villanelles, An Exaltation of Forms, Measure for Measure: An Anthology of Poetic Meters*, and *Choice Words: Writers on Abortion*. Her other works include prosody, essays on poetics, poetry translation, and collaborations with choral music, opera, theater, and dance. Finch's work has been a finalist for the Yale Series of Younger Poets and Foreword Book Award and honored with the Arlt Prize, Sarasvati Award, and Robert Fitzgerald Award. She earned a Ph.D from Stanford University and served for a decade as Director of the Stonecoast MFA Program in Creative Writing. She is based in New York City and offers workshops and performances worldwide. For more information, please visit anniefinch.com

www.ingramcontent.com/pod-product-compliance
Lightning Source LLC
Chambersburg PA
CBHW052208070526
44585CB00017B/2115